inspiration and
motivation for

MUSICIANS

Tamsin King

summersdale

INSPIRATION AND MOTIVATION FOR MUSICIANS

Summersdale Publishers Ltd
46 West Street
Chichester
West Sussex
PO19 1RP
UK

www.summersdale.com

Printed and bound in the Czech Republic

ISBN: 978-1-84953-706-3

Substantial discounts on bulk quantities of Summersdale books are available to corporations, professional associations and other organisations. For details contact Nicky Douglas by telephone: +44 (0) 1243 756902, fax: +44 (0) 1243 786300 or email: nicky@ summersdale.com.

To: ....

From: ....

MUSIC, ONCE ADMITTED TO
THE SOUL, BECOMES A SORT
OF SPIRIT AND NEVER DIES.

EDWARD BULWER-LYTTON

You are the master of your achievements.

Truly there would be reason to go mad were it not for music.

PYOTR ILYICH TCHAIKOVSKY

Emotion can be a source of inspiration. Write music about how you respond to certain events and scenarios. Keep a journal of how different scenarios made you feel and then draw on this when you come to writing music.

THE DAY YOU OPEN YOUR MIND
TO MUSIC, YOU'RE HALFWAY TO
OPENING YOUR MIND TO LIFE.

PETE TOWNSHEND

Make music a part of your everyday life. You could try:

- writing a new melody or lyrics;
- music practice;
- performing in a show;
- listening to music.

A MUSICIAN'S OR ARTIST'S
RESPONSIBILITY IS A SIMPLE ONE,
AND THAT IS, THROUGH YOUR
MUSIC TO TELL THE TRUTH.

TOM MORELLO

Every musician has a reason for playing – what's yours?

Music should
strike fire
from the heart
of man, and
bring tears
from the eyes
of woman.

LUDWIG VAN BEETHOVEN

Play for an audience as you would like to be played for.

WHAT WE PLAY

IS LIFE.

LOUIS ARMSTRONG

Don't forget that playing
an instrument and singing
are both physical activities.
To perform well requires
a certain level of fitness.
Build exercises into your
routine as well as things
to strengthen your core,
particularly if you are a
singer. You could try:

- finger, hand and
  arm exercises;
- breathing techniques;
- yoga.

NEVER UNDERESTIMATE

THE POWER OF PASSION.

EVE SAWYER

Dream the **impossible,** do the **incredible.**

If you're presenting

yourself

with confidence, you
can pull off

pretty much

anything.

KATY PERRY

Whilst classical music is
an art form, it is
also at its heart
a form of entertainment.

ATTEMPT THE IMPOSSIBLE

IN ORDER TO IMPROVE

YOUR WORK.

BETTE DAVIS

If you are rehearsing
as part of a group then
keep talk to a minimum
as it wastes precious
playing time. If a passage
doesn't go particularly
well then keep playing it
until it does go right.

MAKING THE SIMPLE
COMPLICATED IS COMMONPLACE;
MAKING THE COMPLICATED
SIMPLE, AWESOMELY SIMPLE,
THAT'S CREATIVITY.

CHARLES MINGUS

Creativity

inspires

creativity.

We rely more on
enthusiasm
than actual skill.
Whatever you do,
do it
enthusiastically and
people will
like it more.

CHRIS MARTIN

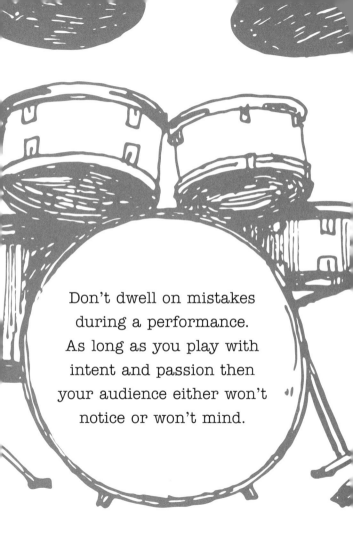

Don't dwell on mistakes during a performance. As long as you play with intent and passion then your audience either won't notice or won't mind.

TO SEND LIGHT INTO
THE DARKNESS OF MEN'S
HEARTS – SUCH IS THE
DUTY OF THE ARTIST.

ROBERT SCHUMANN

Hook your audience in
the first ten seconds
of a performance.

- Smile and greet them
  warmly and it will
  engage them.
- Start the piece strongly
  to set the mood.
- Play with passion. Do
  you like the piece? What
  does it mean to you?

ONLY THOSE WHO HAVE THE
PATIENCE TO DO SIMPLE
THINGS PERFECTLY WILL
ACQUIRE THE SKILLS TO DO
DIFFICULT THINGS EASILY.

FRIEDRICH SCHILLER

No one said it was going to be easy; you'll get there in the end.

One is not
born
a genius, one
becomes
a genius.

SIMONE DE BEAUVOIR

Be direct. If something isn't right during a lesson or rehearsal then address it and work out a solution.

ALL GREAT ACHIEVEMENTS

REQUIRE TIME.

MAYA ANGELOU

Remember the thing that sparked your desire to learn music. Think about it each time you play. Even if you have no intention of practising, take your violin out of its case, stand before the microphone or sit down at the piano and see if you still don't feel like playing.

MUSIC DOESN'T LIE. IF THERE IS SOMETHING TO BE CHANGED IN THIS WORLD, THEN IT CAN ONLY HAPPEN THROUGH MUSIC.

JIMI HENDRIX

Music is everywhere if you just stop and listen.

I take

inspiration

from everything
around me, also

relationships

and friends. And
the inside of my

crazy head.

ELLIE GOULDING

Music should be serious AND
fun, so play with people that
you can have a laugh with.

A PAINTER PAINTS HIS
PICTURES ON CANVAS. BUT
MUSICIANS PAINT THEIR
PICTURES ON SILENCE.

LEOPOLD STOKOWSKI

Seek inspiration from other art forms. The famous novelist Leo Tolstoy wrote a novella based on Beethoven's 'Kreutzer Sonata'. The novella then in turn inspired René François Xavier Prinet's painting of the same name. You could try:

- composing a piece to accompany your favourite novel;
- turning a poem into a song;
- creating a dramatic soundtrack to a film.

THE WISE MUSICIANS ARE
THOSE WHO PLAY WHAT
THEY CAN MASTER.

DUKE ELLINGTON

We are judged by what we finish, not by what we start.

People often say that
motivation
doesn't last. Well,
neither does
bathing
– that's why we
recommend it
daily.

ZIG ZIGLAR

Where possible, have your instrument(s) ready to play. Simply being able to pick something up – rather than spending time setting up – will encourage practice.

OPTIMISM IS THE FAITH
THAT LEADS TO ACHIEVEMENT.
NOTHING CAN BE DONE
WITHOUT HOPE AND
CONFIDENCE.

HELEN KELLER

Vocalise your affirmations to enhance and inspire creativity. By actively voicing your feelings on a subject, you will add drive and passion. For example:

- 'I am confident in my ability as a musician.'
- 'Today I will discover something new.'
- 'Every challenge that presents itself is an opportunity to advance.'

I HATE COMPLACENCY. I PLAY
EVERY GIG AS IF IT COULD
BE MY LAST, THEN I ENJOY
IT MORE THAN EVER.

NIGEL KENNEDY

Make sure that you put **meaning** and **energy** into **everything** that you **practise**.

IT IS NEVER TOO LATE

TO BE WHAT YOU

MIGHT HAVE BEEN.

Start with a primary focus. By beginning practice with clear intentions, you can achieve more in a shorter time frame.

ONE MUST APPROACH MUSIC
WITH A SERIOUS RIGOUR AND,
AT THE SAME TIME, WITH A
GREAT, AFFECTIONATE JOY.

NADIA BOULANGER

Listen to as much music as you can, whether it's a live performance or a recording. Pay attention to what the musicians are doing by listening actively, imagining that you are the one playing the piece.

MUSIC CAN CHANGE THE
WORLD BECAUSE IT CAN
CHANGE PEOPLE.

BONO

Stop and listen to the world.

Ever tried.

Ever failed.

No matter.

Try again.

Fail again.

Fail better.

SAMUEL BECKETT

Allow yourself to make
mistakes; they will
spark creativity.

FIRST YOU MASTER YOUR
INSTRUMENT, THEN YOU
MASTER THE MUSIC; THEN
YOU FORGET ABOUT ALL
THAT AND JUST PLAY.

CHARLIE PARKER

If you need to freshen up your love for creating beautiful sounds, try playing an instrument that you've never tried before. It will either inspire you to continue with it or restore your love of your original chosen instrument.

I WOULD TEACH CHILDREN MUSIC,
PHYSICS AND PHILOSOPHY;
BUT MOST IMPORTANTLY
MUSIC, FOR IN THE PATTERNS
OF MUSIC AND ALL THE ARTS
ARE THE KEYS OF LEARNING.

PLATO

Don't be afraid
to just play.

You can't use up
creativity.
The more you use,
the more
you have.

MAYA ANGELOU

Reinvent a piece that you
wouldn't normally play. If you
play a classical instrument,
try out a piece written
for the electric guitar.

I THINK MUSIC IN ITSELF IS
HEALING. IT'S AN EXPLOSIVE
EXPRESSION OF HUMANITY.
IT'S SOMETHING WE ARE
ALL TOUCHED BY.

BILLY JOEL

Try not to worry if you
suffer from stage fright.
Many successful musicians
do. It just means that you
care and will probably
give a better performance
than if you approach
it with nonchalance.

IF YOU CAN WALK YOU
CAN DANCE. IF YOU CAN
TALK YOU CAN SING.

ZIMBABWEAN PROVERB

Don't lose **faith** in yourself. When you **feel** like quitting, **think** about why you started playing music.

Find out what
your gift
is and
nurture it.

KATY PERRY

Remember to pat yourself
on the back every so
often and acknowledge
when you've done well.

MUSIC IS WHAT FEELINGS
SOUND LIKE.

ANONYMOUS

Work to find your voice. Whether you're just starting out or getting back in the game, don't be afraid to explore sounds. Remember that no one sounds perfect in the beginning.

PEOPLE WANT TO SEE
MUSICIANS SING THINGS
THAT COME FROM THEIR OWN
MIND AND OWN HEART...
RESPONDING TO THE MOMENT.

JOHN MAYER

If you enjoyed playing it, it is not time wasted.

First say to
yourself
what you
would be;
and then
do what you
have to do.

EPICTETUS

Don't let practice become a chore. Set yourself new goals every day and you will start to discover new things with every session.

THE TRUE BEAUTY OF MUSIC
IS THAT IT CONNECTS PEOPLE.
IT CARRIES A MESSAGE,
AND... THE MUSICIANS,
ARE THE MESSENGERS.

ROY AYERS

Confidence helps to dispel
the feeling of stress
before a performance so
psych yourself up by:

- having family and friends
  give you a pep talk;
- keeping a note of your
  achievements so that if you
  feel like you can't perform
  you will be able to remind
  yourself that you can;
- reminding yourself what
  you are trying to achieve.

MUSIC IS ENOUGH FOR A
LIFETIME – BUT A LIFETIME IS
NOT ENOUGH FOR MUSIC.

SERGEI RACHMANINOFF

Discipline is choosing between what you want now and what you want most.

Sometimes you
need to take a
departure
from what you do to
something that's
slightly
different in order
to get inspiration.

TORI AMOS

Use your own experiences
– both good and bad – as
inspiration for your music.

MUSIC CAN BRING A TEAR
TO YOUR EYE. IT CAN MAKE
YOU JUMP OUT OF YOUR
SEAT AND APPLAUD, AND
THAT'S WHY WE'RE HERE.

HAROLD WHEELER

Find ways to relax. It's just as important to build in time to prepare for the pre-show nerves as well as the performance itself. Here are some things you could try:

- compiling a playlist of your favourite music to listen to beforehand;
- yoga or breathing exercises;
- a walk in the fresh air;
- looking at photographs of your favourite moments – whether it's of friends and family, musicians you aspire to be like or from your own past performances.

IN ORDER TO COMPOSE, ALL
YOU NEED TO DO IS REMEMBER
A TUNE THAT NOBODY
ELSE HAS THOUGHT OF.

ROBERT SCHUMANN

Be patient; great sound will come in time.

You may be
disappointed
if you fail, but you
are doomed
if you don't try.

BEVERLY SILLS

Set yourself a goal. Nothing motivates practice more than a looming performance.

A COMPOSER... GOES AROUND
FORCING HIS WILL ON
UNSUSPECTING AIR MOLECULES,
OFTEN WITH THE ASSISTANCE
OF UNSUSPECTING MUSICIANS.

FRANK ZAPPA

If you're singing in rehearsal or a lesson and a high note is approaching that you feel you can't reach, don't dwell on that fact as it will cause tension in your voice and body. Instead try these tips:

- Make a punching motion towards the ground with your fist as you sing the high note.
- Reach up towards the sky if you are worried about reaching a low note.

These psychological motions will help you to achieve the notes without reminding you that you find them challenging.

I PAY NO ATTENTION
WHATEVER TO ANYBODY'S
PRAISE OR BLAME. I SIMPLY
FOLLOW MY OWN FEELINGS.

WOLFGANG AMADEUS MOZART

Don't ever think that you're not good enough.

Sometimes we have
criticism
that is very
constructive.

CHRIS MARTIN

Try to imitate your favourite performer's style (you can even dress up as them if you wish to!).

AFTER SILENCE, THAT WHICH COMES NEAREST TO EXPRESSING THE INEXPRESSIBLE IS MUSIC.

ALDOUS HUXLEY

In order to project your voice so that the whole audience can hear you, try focusing your attention to the back of the auditorium. Imagine that you're singing to the back row and it will help to carry the sound.

MUSIC IS WHAT LIFE

SOUNDS LIKE.

ERIC OLSON

Think back to when you started and how much you've improved.

I don't try to **sound like** anyone but me any more. If **something** is out of my element, I try to **avoid it.**

NORAH JONES

Don't compare yourself to other musicians, only you can make yourself better.

TECHNICALLY, I'M NOT EVEN
A GUITAR PLAYER; ALL I PLAY
IS TRUTH AND EMOTION.

JIMI HENDRIX

Even if you are not
rehearsing, you can practise.
Every time that you
listen to a piece of music,
imagine yourself playing
or singing along to it. Your
muscles will automatically
remember how it feels to
play/sing and this will help
you the next time you do
pick up your instrument.

MUSIC IS THE VOICE THAT TELLS
US THAT THE HUMAN RACE IS
GREATER THAN IT KNOWS.

NAPOLÉON BONAPARTE

Never give up on something you really want.

Music gives a soul to the universe, wings to the mind, flight to the imagination, and life to everything.

PLATO

If the idea of a big performance seems unnerving, then start small by performing one piece for friends and family.

IT ISN'T WHERE YOU CAME
FROM, IT'S WHERE YOU'RE
GOING THAT COUNTS.

ELLA FITZGERALD

Start practice, an audition
or a performance in the
right mindset. Listen to
a piece that inspires you
or that reminds you of
how you aspire to play.

MUSIC HELPS YOU FIND THE
TRUTHS YOU MUST BRING INTO
THE REST OF YOUR LIFE.

ALANIS MORISSETTE

Don't wish for it. Work for it.

Songwriting is a very mysterious process. It feels like creating something from nothing. It's something I don't feel like I really control.

TRACY CHAPMAN

Look for new ways to approach your music tuition, such as taking a class or trying to play a new style.

WHERE WORDS FAIL,

MUSIC SPEAKS.

HANS CHRISTIAN ANDERSEN

When singing, remember
to expel all the air from
your lungs before taking
another breath. If you try
to save it, you will end
up feeling light-headed.

EVERY TIME I GET UP AND
SING FOR PEOPLE, I GET SUCH
A HIGH. I JUST WANT TO
DO IT AGAIN AND AGAIN.

PIXIE LOTT

Every musician has a need for an audience.

No matter who you are,
no matter
what you did, no
matter where you've
come from,
you can always
change, become a
better version
of yourself.

MADONNA

Consider one of your usual practice routines. Could you improve it? If so, then do.

WITHOUT MUSIC, LIFE WOULD BE A MISTAKE.

FRIEDRICH NIETZSCHE

Rehearse with a metronome.
It may seem boring but
timing is a key aspect of
great musicality. It will
impact your ability to
perform as a group or
with accompaniment.

WHEN THINGS GO WRONG,

DON'T GO WITH THEM.

ELVIS PRESLEY

Push yourself
a bit harder.

Music is
forever;
music should
grow
and mature with you.

PAUL SIMON

Try putting words to
instrumental melodies, to help
with the phrasing. It could be
a short sentence repeated over
and over, or a shopping list!

MUSIC COMES FROM A
PLACE WE DON'T KNOW.

CHRIS MARTIN

When singing, it is important that you maintain a good posture. Imagine that you have a string attached at the top of your head to the ceiling. It will create an upright but relaxed stance.

EVERY ARTIST WAS

FIRST AN AMATEUR.

RALPH WALDO EMERSON

If you don't give up today, tomorrow you will do better.

Don't over-rehearse. If there are fewer opportunities to sharpen your piece then each session will be more focused.

MUSICIANS DON'T RETIRE;
THEY STOP WHEN THERE'S
NO MORE MUSIC IN THEM.

LOUIS ARMSTRONG

If you're interested in finding out more about our books, find us on Facebook at Summersdale Publishers and follow us on Twitter at @Summersdale.

WWW.SUMMERSDALE.COM